Decoding Startup India

A Chartered Accountant's Strategic Playbook

By

CA MEGHA JAIN

★ ★ ★ ★

Disclaimer: No one make representation or warranties with respect to the accuracy, applicability, or completeness of the contents. The author shall in no event be held liable for any loss or other damages, including but not limited to special, incidental, consequential, or other damages. The information presented in this publication is compiled from sources believed to be accurate. However, author assume no responsibility for errors or omissions. The information in this publication is not intended to replace or substitute professional advice. This handbook is meant for associates and professional connects of the author.

ACKNOWLEDGEMENTS

- I would like to express my sincere gratitude to **Mr. Gaurav Arora** for their invaluable guidance and support during the writing of this book.

- I am also thankful to my Family, especially my husband **Mr Punith Jain** & son **Mstr. Anay Jain**, for their constant encouragement and understanding.

- I am also thankful to all **my staff members**, who continuously supporting me, by handling all operational work with a dedication and encouragement.

- A special thanks to the **Startup India initiative** and the **Ministry of Commerce and Industry** for their efforts in promoting entrepreneurship in India.

PREFACE

When I first stepped into the world of startup registrations and 80-IAC certifications, I didn't find a roadmap—I had to build one. While most practitioners remained focused on traditional compliance work, I saw a gap: promising startups were leaving serious value on the table simply because their Chartered Accountants weren't aware, equipped, or willing to step into this niche.

This book is not a manual. It's a practitioner's perspective—shaped by on-ground execution, trial-and-error learning, and a relentless focus on outcomes. Over the past few years, I've worked closely with founders across sectors and stages, navigating DPIIT recognition and the 80-IAC tax exemption with a clear, process-driven approach. Along the way, I've built a system that works, even in cases where others failed.

If you're a Chartered Accountant reading this, my purpose is straightforward: I want to bring you into a niche that's high-impact, under-served, and entirely within your reach—if approached with precision and intent. Whether you wish to collaborate, refer, or simply understand what it takes to play at this level, this book is your insider look.

This book adheres to the ethical guidelines of ICAI. Let's raise the bar for what the CA profession can do for India's startup ecosystem.

– CA Megha Jain

ABOUT THE AUTHOR

CA Megha Jain is a highly experienced and dedicated Chartered Accountant (CA) with over **14 years of expertise** in the fields of **taxation, compliance, auditing**, and **startup advisory services**. With a proven track record in helping startups, small businesses, and established organizations navigate the complex world of taxation and business regulations, she has earned a reputation for her commitment to delivering clear, actionable, and effective solutions.

Her **passion for empowering startups** and entrepreneurs to thrive in a competitive business environment has driven her to specialize in **business registrations, tax planning**, and **compliance management**. She is known for her practical and client-focused approach, using her deep knowledge of Indian tax laws to help businesses save taxes, maximize growth, and ensure legal compliance.

CA Megha Jain works closely with **startups** across a wide range of industries, assisting them with

- **Company Formation,**

- **Tax Planning & Maximizing Benefits,**

- **Stay Compliant with Government Regulations**

- **Strategic Advice**

- **And Many more...**

With her **hands-on expertise** and thorough understanding of the unique challenges faced by entrepreneurs, she provides customized solutions that are both cost-effective and efficient.

Educational Background:

CA Megha Jain holds a degree in Commerce from Kurukshetra University and is a member of the Institute of Chartered Accountants of India (ICAI) and a member of the Institute of Company Secretary of India (ICSI). Additionally, CA Megha Jain has completed various specialized diploma & certification courses in Various Taxation, Forensic Accounting & Fraud Detection, Information System Audit, and Banking Audits, etc.

Currently, Megha Jain is the founder of J Megha & Co., a Chartered Accountant Firm that was established in 2018 (Deemed 2012) in the heart of Bengaluru, India.

Publications and Speaking Engagements:

Beyond her professional work, CA Megha Jain is also an active speaker and educator, regularly conducting workshops, seminars and webinars to spread awareness about the importance of financial planning and tax compliance. She firmly believes that a **strong financial foundation** and a commitment to **legal compliance** are the keys to long-term business success.

She is also the author of ***Beyond the Incorporation***, a practical guide that helps entrepreneurs navigate the registration, post-registration compliance landscape & Tax Saving Strategy with clarity and confidence.

This book is the culmination of CA Megha Jain's focused experience in the niche domain of startup registration and 80-IAC certification. It offers actionable insights not to startups, but to fellow Chartered Accountants—highlighting real-world strategies, execution frameworks, and lessons learned from handling high-stakes cases. Through this book, she aims to empower CAs to recognize the untapped potential in this advisory space, avoid common missteps, and either enter the niche themselves or confidently collaborate with an established expert. It's not just about compliance—it's about positioning, results, and next-level client value.

THIS BOOK IS FOR 

This book is for Chartered Accountants who are either:

- Unaware of the Startup India ecosystem and the Section 80-IAC tax exemption opportunity,

- Aware, but unsure how to execute the process confidently, or

- Looking to collaborate or refer clients in this niche without taking on the execution risk themselves.

It is not an educational guide for founders or students. It is a positioning playbook—meant to:

- Showcase real-world wins,

- Demonstrate domain authority, and

- Invite other CAs to either partner with or learn from a proven expert in this domain.

In short, this book is for fellow CAs who should walk away thinking, *"Megha Jain has mastered this space. I'd rather bring her in than figure it out myself."*

– CA Megha Jain

TABLE OF CONTENTS

CHAPTER 1

INTRODUCTION: WHY I CHOSE TO SPECIALIZE IN STARTUPS

When I began my CA Practicing journey, I was surrounded by peers immersed in GST, TDS, and statutory filings. The traditional path was well laid out, yet I found myself asking: Is that all there is for us?

It was during a client interaction that I first came across the Startup India scheme. A young founder, full of ambition but clueless about government incentives, walked into my office. That conversation changed the trajectory of my practice.

I realized startups are not just businesses—they're economic catalysts. Yet most of them were either unaware of or denied access to tax exemptions like 80-IAC. Worse, their advisors were not even considering these possibilities. That gap became my opportunity. I immersed myself in understanding DPIIT recognition, 80-IAC certification, and the interlink between policy and execution. I learned what works, what fails, and what the Inter-Ministerial Board (IMB) really expects.

This niche matters because it sits at the intersection of government policy, founder ambition, and strategic tax planning. With the Indian government aggressively promoting innovation through the Startup India initiative, benefits like DPIIT recognition and Section 80-IAC tax exemptions offer founders massive incentives—yet most remain unaware or unsupported.

For Chartered Accountants, this creates a high-impact advisory opportunity: not just to guide startups through compliance, but to help them unlock tangible tax savings, attract investment, and scale faster. In a profession crowded with routine work, this niche offers a forward-looking, value-driven path.

This book is the product of that journey. This is not a guidebook. It is a real-world playbook. If you're a Chartered Accountant looking to go beyond the basics and offer real value to startups, consider this your roadmap.

CHAPTER 2

NAVIGATING THE NUANCES OF STARTUP REGISTRATION

Advanced DPIIT Criteria and Interpretations

The Department for Promotion of Industry and Internal Trade (DPIIT) under the Ministry of Commerce and Industry plays a pivotal role in startup recognition in India. While the baseline criteria for recognition include factors such as company age, type of entity, turnover limits, and innovation-driven purpose, interpreting these standards in complex startup scenarios requires finesse.

For example, a company incorporated as a Private Limited entity is eligible, but challenges often arise when startups undergo restructuring, mergers, or pivot their business models. In such cases, professionals must interpret DPIIT guidelines in the context of evolving operations. Innovation and scalability, the two pillars of eligibility, must be demonstrated not merely through a business plan but via measurable proof like patents, early traction, or industry disruption.

Advanced interpretations also focus on hybrid models (like product-plus-service combinations), international holding structures, and secondary offices. Recognizing how DPIIT evaluates such blended business models can help startups position themselves more effectively.

Optimizing Legal Structures for DPIIT Compliance

Choosing the right legal entity is crucial. While LLPs and Private Limited Companies are eligible, a Private Limited Company is often preferable due to the scalability of shareholding and ease of compliance with investor expectations.

Advanced planning also involves:

- Structuring cap tables to accommodate future ESOPs and VC rounds.

- Establishing clear Founder Agreements and IP ownership clauses.

- Ensuring that group entities don't inadvertently disqualify the startup due to consolidated turnover exceeding ₹100 crore.

It's recommended to use compliance management tools and seek periodic legal reviews to ensure continued eligibility.

Mastering the Startup India Portal: Advanced Techniques

The Startup India Portal serves as the central hub for startup registration and DPIIT recognition. While the process seems straightforward, optimizing submissions for approval requires strategy:

- Tailor your business description using keywords that align with DPIIT focus sectors.

- Upload evidence of innovation (product demos, white papers, IP filings).

- Use concise but compelling language in problem statements and solutions to stand out in the evaluation process.

Additionally, startups should keep all documents ready in proper formats—such as Incorporation Certificate, PAN, and pitch decks—before initiating registration to minimize delays.

Mitigating Risks in Startup Registration

Startups face several risks during and after the DPIIT recognition process:

- Eligibility misinterpretation: Often, startups misjudge their innovation quotient or assume eligibility despite being subsidiaries of larger entities.

- Documentation issues: Mismatches between documents and online entries often lead to rejection.

- Post-recognition compliance: DPIIT status can be revoked if a startup fails to maintain compliance with innovation or operational benchmarks.

Risk mitigation strategies include:

- Conducting a pre-recognition eligibility audit.

- Engaging professionals for document preparation and portal navigation.

- Setting up internal compliance checkpoints.

Summary

Startup registration in India has matured into a process that demands more than just fulfilling checkboxes. A deep understanding of DPIIT's evolving expectations, a strategic legal foundation, and proactive compliance can significantly increase the chances of successful and sustained startup recognition.

CHAPTER 3

ADVANCED STRATEGIES FOR 80IAC CERTIFICATION

Deep Dive into 80IAC Eligibility Criteria

Section 80-IAC of the Income Tax Act, 1961, offers a powerful incentive to eligible startups: a 100% tax exemption on profits for any three consecutive assessment years out of First Ten years from incorporation. However, the eligibility criteria are nuanced and often misunderstood.

The key conditions include:

- The entity must be a Private Limited Company or LLP.

- It must be incorporated after April 1, 2016 but before April 1, 2030.

- Turnover must not exceed ₹100 crore in any of the years since incorporation.

- It must hold DPIIT recognition as an eligible startup.

- The startup must be engaged in innovation, development, or improvement of products/processes/services, or be a scalable business model with a high potential for employment or wealth creation.

Common mistakes include applying for 80IAC without DPIIT recognition or misrepresenting revenue to stay under the turnover cap. CAs and consultants must carefully audit the business model and financials before advising on eligibility.

Maximizing 80IAC Benefits: Advanced Techniques

To extract full value from the 80IAC provision, timing and strategy are critical.

- **Strategic Year Selection**: Since the exemption applies to three consecutive assessment years, it is essential to delay claiming the benefit until the startup is profitable. This requires forecasting and financial modeling to identify the most profitable future window.

- **Restructuring Shareholding Patterns**: Clean cap tables, ESOP pools, and clear shareholder agreements help avoid scrutiny during evaluation. DPIIT and IMB often raise red flags over complex or layered ownership.

- **IP Documentation:** Demonstrating innovation through provisional patents, R&D records, or published research boosts the application.

- **Audit Trail Maintenance**: Maintain thorough documentation of revenue, client contracts, tech development timelines, and employee count to support your claims during scrutiny by the Inter-Ministerial Board (IMB).

Navigating the 80IAC Application Process: Expert Insights

The 80IAC process involves submission through the Startup India Portal, followed by IMB evaluation. Key submission components include:

- Form-1 Submission with business overview, innovation summary, and financials.

- Pitch deck or business plan tailored to show scalability and innovation.

- Supporting documents like Incorporation Certificate, PAN, and annual filings.

Expert insights:

- Tailor your pitch to reflect quantifiable impact—jobs created, industries disrupted, or user adoption metrics.

- Anticipate scrutiny on related-party transactions, foreign ownership, and group entities.

- Involve a CA with experience in 80IAC certification to avoid technical rejections.

In case of rejection, startups can resubmit with corrections or file a representation to DPIIT with additional documentation.

Mitigating Risks and Ensuring Long-Term Compliance

Securing 80IAC approval is only the beginning. Sustaining eligibility and protecting the benefit require robust compliance.

- **Avoid retrospective disqualification**: Any violation of conditions—such as exceeding turnover or changing business activity—can lead to loss of benefits and penalties.

- **Regular compliance checks**: Implement quarterly internal reviews for turnover, shareholder structure, and operational focus.

- **Documentation retention**: Maintain five-year records for all financials and filings in case of future audits by the IT Department.

Startups should also stay alert to regulatory updates, as thresholds and deadlines under DPIIT and IT Act may evolve over time.

Summary

The 80IAC certification is a cornerstone tax incentive for Indian startups. To fully leverage this opportunity, startups must approach the process with strategic timing, deep understanding of criteria, and meticulous documentation. With the right advisory support and proactive compliance, the benefits can translate into significant tax savings and investor confidence.

INTEGRATING 80IAC WITH BROADER TAX STRATEGIES

Optimizing Tax Incidence for Startups

While Section 80IAC provides a powerful exemption, it's only one component of a well-planned tax strategy. Startups should seek to minimize total tax incidence across multiple fronts:

- **Deferred Revenue Recognition:** If a startup expects to invoke 80IAC in future years, it may structure contracts to defer revenue—within permissible accounting standards—to optimize the exemption window.

- **Capital Structure Planning:** Choosing between equity, convertible instruments, or venture debt affects tax obligations. For example, interest payments on venture debt are tax-deductible but may dilute exemption benefits if poorly timed.

- **ESOP Design:** Employee Stock Option Plans are critical in startups but come with complex tax implications. Planning for ESOP issuance post-80IAC period, or aligning vesting schedules with profit years, can significantly reduce tax burdens.

- **Input Tax Credits (ITC)** under GST should also be efficiently managed to prevent cascading tax burdens, especially for startups operating in both B2B and B2C domains.

Navigating Regulatory Changes and Updates

India's startup policy landscape is dynamic. Over the past five years, changes in turnover limits, timelines for eligibility, and procedural requirements have had significant implications for 80IAC and DPIIT recognition.

Professionals working with startups must:

- Monitor Finance Acts annually for changes to Sections 80IAC, 56(2)(viib), and related clauses.

- Keep track of notifications and circulars from DPIIT, CBDT, and MCA.

- Join or follow startup-focused networks like TiE, NASSCOM, and legal/CA communities to stay ahead of changes.

Staying updated is not only essential for new applicants but also for startups that have already claimed benefits and need to maintain eligibility.

Leveraging Technology for Efficient Compliance

Technology can drastically reduce compliance burden and improve accuracy in financial reporting:

- **Automated Accounting and Tax Tools:** Use cloud-based software (e.g., Zoho Books, QuickBooks, TallyPrime) with integrated tax modules to track exempt income separately, generate GST returns, and issue compliant invoices.

- **Cap Table Management:** Tools like Carta or Qapita can manage shareholder records, ESOP allocations, and investor rights—all of which are scrutinized in 80IAC audits.

- **Compliance Dashboards:** Building a simple internal dashboard using Excel or a business intelligence tool can help monitor turnover, exemption utilization, and compliance deadlines.

- **Digital Documentation Repositories:** Use secure cloud storage to organize key documents—pitch decks, IP filings, financial statements, and shareholder agreements—for easy access during audits or IMB evaluations.

Integrating these tools not only ensures compliance but also demonstrates to authorities and investors that the startup operates with transparency and precision.

Summary

A strong tax strategy goes beyond 80IAC by aligning financial decisions, regulatory awareness, and technology adoption. Startups that proactively manage their tax footprint, structure their financial instruments wisely, and use modern compliance tools are better positioned for sustained growth and risk-free audits.

CHAPTER 5

CASE STUDIES – EXPERT INSIGHTS AND PRACTICAL SOLUTIONS

Complex 80IAC Cases and Resolutions

Case 1: DPIIT-Recognized but 80IAC Rejected

Background: A Bengaluru-based SaaS startup received DPIIT recognition and had filed for 80IAC claiming innovation and scalability. Despite early-stage funding and revenue traction, the IMB rejected the application.

Problem: The startup's pitch lacked a clear demonstration of innovation. Their business was essentially a CRM product for SMEs—perceived as commoditized.

Resolution:

- The CA helped them build a stronger case for innovation, including R&D documentation, UI/UX patents filed, and scalability metrics.

- The revised application focused on unique tech integrations and international market expansion.

- The startup was approved on resubmission after 3 months.

Lesson: DPIIT recognition is not a guarantee for 80IAC. IMB approval requires a deeper justification of innovation, not just business growth.

Case 2: Startup with Holding Company Abroad

Background: A D2C startup incorporated in India was DPIIT-recognized and applied for 80IAC. However, a majority of its equity was held by a Delaware-based parent company.

Problem: Questions arose about the Indian startup's independence, given its foreign ownership.

Resolution:

- The advisory team presented a clear legal separation of business functions, proving the Indian entity had control over product development and revenue.

- Detailed financial segregation was provided.

- The IMB granted approval after verifying the independence of operations.

Lesson: Foreign holding structures aren't automatic disqualifiers—but require strong documentation to prove the Indian entity's independent innovation role.

Optimizing 80IAC for High-Growth Startups

High-growth startups must make strategic decisions to maximize the value of the 80IAC exemption:

- **Case in Point:** A fintech firm crossed ₹80 crore turnover in Year 4 but hadn't claimed 80IAC yet. They projected ₹20 crore profit in Years 5–7.

- **Strategy:** Their CA advised them to delay claiming the exemption until Year 5 to capture the full benefit during profitable years. A revised business plan was submitted highlighting projected profits and scalability.

- **Result:** The startup saved over ₹6 crore in taxes over three years.

Takeaway: Use advanced financial modeling to time your 80IAC claim. Don't rush into the exemption in low-earning years.

Preventing and Resolving 80IAC Disputes

80IAC approvals can be challenged by the tax department in scrutiny assessments or future audits. Common causes:

- Misreporting turnover thresholds.

- Using the same exemption in multiple related entities.

- Improper selection of the three-year window.

Case: Notice After 80IAC Approval

An e-commerce startup received IMB approval but was issued a notice during assessment, questioning whether the exemption was claimed in the correct years.

Resolution:

- Their advisor had maintained detailed audit trails, including board meeting minutes, financial projections, and investor communications justifying the exemption years.

- The dispute was closed without penalties after proper representation.

Best Practices:

- Keep all exemption-related decisions minute formally.

- Cross-verify Form ITR filings to reflect exempt income properly.

- Train your finance team or CA to handle exemptions and tax notices defensively.

Summary

Real-world cases show that 80IAC success depends on more than paperwork. Startups must understand regulatory nuances, structure their business transparently, and maintain solid documentation to withstand scrutiny. With strategic guidance and robust compliance, even complex or high-risk cases can achieve favourable outcomes.

CHAPTER 6

THE FUTURE OF 80IAC AND STARTUP INCENTIVES

Anticipating Policy Changes

The startup ecosystem in India is undergoing continuous transformation. As the government pushes for economic self-reliance and digital innovation, incentive policies like 80IAC are likely to evolve. Key trends that may shape the future include:

- **Extension of Eligibility Period:** With the original 80IAC window closing in 2030, industry bodies are lobbying for an extension to support a new generation of startups post-pandemic.

- **Sector-Based Incentives:** Future 80IAC-style benefits may be reserved or modified for high-impact sectors like DeepTech, ClimateTech, Agritech, and HealthTech.

- **Performance-Linked Exemptions:** Policymakers may introduce conditional exemptions linked to job creation, exports, or IP generation rather than just DPIIT recognition.

Startups and advisors must track policy reviews and contribute to consultations where possible. Being early adopters of policy changes provides both strategic and compliance advantages.

The Role of CAs in Shaping Policy

Chartered Accountants (CAs) and legal professionals are increasingly becoming policy influencers, not just advisors. Their role is expanding in three key areas:

- **Representation and Advocacy:** CAs can submit feedback to the CBDT, DPIIT, or MCA during draft policy consultations. Representing startup pain points helps align future policies with ground realities.

- **Standard-Setting:** Through ICAI and professional networks, CAs help define best practices for compliance, audit, and valuation, directly impacting how policies are interpreted and applied.

- **Knowledge Dissemination:** CAs who build expertise in startup taxation and regulatory support often lead workshops, webinars, and author guidance notes that influence thousands of early-stage businesses.

In short, the future of startup policy is not just shaped by bureaucrats—it's informed by professionals who work at the intersection of regulation and innovation.

Emerging Opportunities for CAs

The startup sector offers tremendous scope for diversified, high-value professional services. Opportunities include:

- **Valuation Services:** With increased scrutiny under Angel Tax (Section 56(2)(viib)), professionally certified valuations are critical—especially for funding rounds and foreign investments.

- **Virtual CFO Services:** Startups often outsource financial management. CAs with tech-savvy operations can provide scalable services like compliance dashboards, cash flow forecasting, and investor reporting.

- **Startup-Focused Tax Planning:** Crafting tax strategies that combine 80IAC with other benefits (such as R&D deductions, SEZ benefits, or international tax treaties) positions CAs as strategic partners.

- **Advisory for Global Expansion:** As more Indian startups expand abroad, there's a rising demand for international tax structuring, cross-border compliance, and transfer pricing expertise.

CAs who proactively upskill in startup finance, technology adoption, and international taxation will be best positioned to capture this growing market.

Summary

The landscape of startup incentives is expanding and evolving. For startups, this means new opportunities—but also a need for sharper compliance and strategic planning. For CAs and advisors, the future lies in thought leadership, policy influence, and embracing tech-enabled services to meet the complex needs of high-growth ventures.

CHAPTER 7

THE STARTUP LANDSCAPE—A NEW FRONTIER FOR CAS

India is now the third-largest startup ecosystem in the world. From fintech to agritech, edtech to deep tech, innovation is no longer limited to elite metros. The government's Startup India initiative was a game-changer. It aimed to promote innovation, attract capital, and reduce regulatory friction.

Two major pillars of this scheme are DPIIT recognition and the Section 80-IAC tax holiday.

- DPIIT recognition helps startups access funding, faster compliance routes, and credibility.
- 80-IAC offers a three-year tax holiday under certain conditions.

Together, they form a potent advantage for eligible startups, yet most are unaware of it. where Chartered Accountants should be playing a bigger role. The average startup doesn't just need a tax filer. They need a strategic advisor who understands both their ambition and the ecosystem they are navigating. Unfortunately, many CAs stay away from this domain due to perceived complexity or the real gap and where your value can multiply.

If you know how to assess eligibility, frame the innovation correctly, and navigate the DPIIT and IMB approval process, you don't just file returns. You unlock scale for your client. You become irreplaceable.

CHAPTER 8

FROM POLICY TO PRACTICE—REAL-WORLD EXECUTION

It's a time to move beyond theory. The real power of DPIIT and 80-IAC lies in how they are executed. Here are anonymized examples from my practice that highlight the nuance of this work:

Case 1: The Innovation Reframe A client in the IT sector was initially rejected for DPIIT recognition. The issue?

Their application lacked depth on innovation.

We did not change the business we changed the story. We reframed their use of tech for last-mile optimization, aligned it with DPIIT language, and got it approved.

Case 2: A Second Chance at 80-IAC A tech startup was rejected for 80-IAC before they approached me. They had the tech, but failed to explain how it was unique.

We built a detailed submission, benchmarked it against prior IMB-approved cases, and positioned it as a sectoral first. They were approved.

Case 3: Narrative-Driven Turnaround A women-led firm received DPIIT recognition within 5 working days. Why?

Because we didn't treat it like a formality. We wove their innovation into a larger story of social impact, NEP alignment, and digital inclusivity. The recognition helped them close their seed round.

"DPIIT recognition and 80-IAC certification aren't mere checkbox exercises—they demand strategic articulation of a startup's innovation story and precise execution of documentation. It's not just about meeting eligibility criteria; it's about presenting the business in a way that aligns with policy intent and demonstrates real innovation."

A key insight from my practice is that rejections are not failures—they're data points. Each one reveals what the authorities prioritize, helping refine narratives and strengthen future applications. Over time, this iterative learning loop has helped me build a high-success-rate approach grounded in real-world execution.

These are not 'filing' exercises. They are strategic engagements. Each case taught me that the IMB and DPIIT are looking not just for form compliance, but genuine innovation, backed by clarity and conviction.

CHAPTER 9

WHY MANY AVOID THIS SPACE—AND WHY I STAYED

Why don't more CAs enter the startup certification space?

The short answer? Risk, complexity, and ambiguity.

Most CAs fear the uncertainty in dealing with the DPIIT portal or the IMB's discretionary power. The rejection rate can be intimidating. And without a clear checklist or SOP from the authorities, it feels like guesswork.

But here what I learned early: *Every rejection is a data point.*

My counter-view: "High trust, high ticket, long-term clients."

I built internal SOPs, checklists, and industry-specific playbooks. I started seeing patterns which sectors got easier approvals, what kind of narratives worked, what documentation stood out. I started building a system around an unstructured process.

Today, my practice operates on precision. I don't just submit documents; I submit dossiers tailored to match DPIIT's framework and IMB's expectations. And every approval refines that system further.

Where others saw risk, I saw a niche. Where others saw complexity, I found a moat. That mindset has made all the difference.

CHAPTER 10

HOW CAs CAN CONTRIBUTE TO INDIA'S STARTUP GROWTH

Chartered Accountants are uniquely positioned to help startups go beyond compliance. Your role isn't limited to TDS and GST filings. You have the potential to be strategic growth partners. But for that, we need to step into the advisory zone; especially in emerging areas like startup certifications.

Startups don't know what they don't know. Most are unaware that they could be saving lakhs in taxes under 80-IAC. Or that DPIIT recognition can help them raise funds or participate in government tenders.

Even if you don't want to take on execution, your awareness can make you more valuable. By identifying eligible clients, referring them to specialists, or simply guiding them on possibilities, you position yourself as a strategic thinker.

Ways CAs can plug in:
- As advisors
- As collaborators (even if not experts)
- As ecosystem allies (via incubators, events, online content)

The CA profession is at a crossroads. Those who stay purely transactional will be replaced by automation. Those who embrace advisory, especially in niche verticals like startups, will rise. We don't need more service providers. We need ecosystem allies. Be one."

CHAPTER 11

BUILDING A NICHE—LESSONS FROM MY PRACTICE

This chapter is for the CA who wants more.

I didn't build this niche practice with a team. I built it with systems, clarity, and obsession with value. And here are the biggest lessons I've learned:

1. **Focus Wins:** When you go deep instead of wide, clients notice. Referrals come automatically.
2. **Narrative Matters:** Most applications fail not on merit, but on messaging. Learn how to shape the story.
3. **Rejection Is Feedback:** Every "no" is an insight into how to get to "yes".
4. **Build Playbooks:** Systemize what works. Reuse frameworks. Don't reinvent every time.
5. **Stay Visible:** Share your insights on LinkedIn. Talk to peers. The more visible your expertise, the more you attract the right work.

The real transformation in my journey came when I shifted my mindset from being a service provider to becoming a solution architect.

Instead of merely offering compliance support, I began designing outcomes—structured, strategic, and repeatable.

My system evolved with four core pillars:

- a seamless client onboarding process that filters eligibility early,
- a documentation strategy that anticipates queries,
- a narrative-building method that aligns the startup's innovation with policy language, and
- a rejection-handling approach that treats every 'no' as input for refining our SOPs.

What truly sustained this practice, though, was consistency in delivery, credibility in communication, and sharp focus on this niche—without dilution. This isn't a path of volume, but of value. And let me say it clearly: this path is open for every CA— but only a few will walk it.

Whether you want to replicate this model, or simply collaborate, the future of our profession lies in depth, not breadth. You don't need 100 clients. You need 10 that trust you to deliver transformation."

CHAPTER 12

OUTSOURCING IN STARTUP COMPLIANCE – STRATEGIC SUPPORT, NOT A SHORTCUT

In the evolving world of startups, where agility, compliance, and specialization intersect, outsourcing has emerged as a powerful strategy—when approached with responsibility, transparency, and adherence to ethical norms. As a practicing Chartered Accountant, I have seen how carefully considered outsourcing can enhance service delivery, optimize time, and ultimately serve clients more effectively, especially in niche areas like DPIIT recognition and 80-IAC certification.

Why Consider Outsourcing?

Startups often operate under tight timelines and seek rapid compliance support, but the regulatory framework—particularly around 80-IAC—is both intricate and evolving. For many Chartered Accountants who are either building their practice or not fully specialized in this space, outsourcing certain aspects of the process can offer several advantages:

- **Access to Specialized Knowledge:** DPIIT and 80-IAC require deep familiarity with specific eligibility conditions, documentation standards, pitch presentations, and communication with inter-ministerial boards. Outsourcing to specialists can ensure accuracy and efficiency.

- **Scalability and Speed:** With outsourcing, firms can serve more clients without compromising on quality or missing deadlines. This is especially valuable during peak tax seasons or when a sudden influx of startup clients occurs.

- **Cost-Efficiency:** Rather than building an internal team for an area that may not yet be a core offering, outsourcing allows for cost-effective expansion of services.

- **Learning Opportunity:** Collaborating with experts provides a learning curve for practitioners. Over time, some CAs transition from outsourcing to building their own niche offerings with confidence.

Ethical Considerations and ICAI Guidelines

Outsourcing in itself is not unethical. However, it **must be conducted within the framework of ICAI's Code of Ethics**, particularly the following principles:

- **Client Consent:** It is essential to inform the client clearly and obtain their explicit consent before involving a third party in any part of the engagement.

- **Confidentiality:** Client information shared with outsourced partners must be protected. NDAs and confidentiality agreements should be standard practice.

- **Due Diligence in Selection:** The outsourced service provider must be competent, qualified, and aligned with ICAI's professional and ethical expectations.

- **Transparency:** The primary responsibility for the quality of work rests with the CA. One must never present outsourced work as their own without proper supervision and review.

- **No Commission-Based Referrals:** As per ICAI regulations, practitioners must not enter into fee-sharing or commission-based arrangements with non-members for client acquisition or service delivery.

Outsourcing—A Strategic Tool for Collaboration

For CAs who are new to startup consulting or are considering entering this niche, outsourcing offers a bridge. Rather than declining engagements due to limited bandwidth or technical gaps, collaborating with specialists allows you to retain the client relationship, grow your portfolio, and expand gradually.

In my own practice, I have partnered with firms and practitioners across India—either as a consultant or implementation specialist—always under clear, ethical boundaries. These collaborations have not only deepened trust but have also created a mutually beneficial ecosystem where we all grow.

Conclusion: Responsible Growth through Collaboration

Outsourcing is not about giving away responsibility—it is about **extending capability**. When handled professionally and ethically, it enables CAs to serve clients better, maintain quality, and explore new verticals without compromising on integrity.

As more of us choose to embrace the startup domain, outsourcing can become a strategic ally—**not as a crutch, but as a catalyst** for building expertise and delivering value.

Appendix 1

Detailed Analysis of Key Court Decisions and Case Laws

While Section 80IAC is relatively new, a number of judicial precedents and departmental clarifications around startup taxation, innovation definitions, and eligibility interpretations are worth noting.

1.1 ITAT Ruling: Nature of Innovation Must Be Evident

- Case: XYZ Innovations Pvt. Ltd. vs. Income Tax Officer (Fictitious for illustration)

- Context: The company claimed 80IAC exemption but was denied on grounds of offering a "non-innovative service."

- Observation: The Tribunal ruled that mere digital delivery of a service does not constitute innovation unless substantial improvement or IP is involved.

- Lesson: A documented innovation—via patent filing, proprietary algorithms, or R&D expenditure—significantly strengthens the case.

1.2 CBDT Circular – 56(2)(viib) Angel Tax Clarifications

- Relevance: Several DPIIT-recognized startups faced scrutiny under Angel Tax despite 80IAC approval.

- Update: The CBDT clarified that DPIIT-recognized startups are exempt from Angel Tax scrutiny, provided they file Form 2 with requisite declarations.

- Lesson: Always ensure proper filings and maintain correspondence with DPIIT to avoid tax conflicts.

1.3 Supreme Court View on Business Model Substance

- Case: McDowell & Co. vs. Commercial Tax Officer (1985)

- Though not startup-specific, this landmark case emphasized that substance must prevail over form in tax matters.

- Implication: Structuring a startup solely to qualify for 80IAC—without true innovation—can attract future scrutiny.

APPENDIX 2

COMPREHENSIVE GUIDE TO DPIIT AND IMB PROCEDURES

2.1 DPIIT Recognition – Document Checklist

- Certificate of Incorporation
- PAN of the entity
- Brief write-up of the business model
- Evidence of innovation (patent, research publication, MVP)
- Website or product video links
- Directors' details

2.2 IMB Evaluation for 80IAC – Common Queries

- "Explain how your model is innovative."
- "How is your product/service scalable?"
- "What proof exists for customer validation or early adoption?"

2.3 Best Practices

- Ensure consistent narrative across pitch deck, write-up, and website.
- Keep financials audited and up to date.
- Use startup-focused legal advisors to draft accurate declarations.

APPENDIX 3

PRACTICAL TOOLS & INSIGHTS

This section offers distilled, policy-aligned insights to help Chartered Accountants and stakeholders understand the practical application of Startup India benefits. The intention is not to guide step-by-step execution but to provide a reliable reference for eligibility, evaluation, and opportunity areas within the Startup India framework.

3.1. DPIIT Eligibility Checklist

(As per official Startup India guidelines)

To qualify as a DPIIT-recognized startup, an entity must meet the following conditions:

- **Entity Type:** Must be a Private Limited Company, Registered Partnership Firm, or LLP.

- **Age of the Entity:** Should not exceed 10 years from the date of incorporation.

- **Turnover Cap:** Turnover should not exceed ₹100 crore in any financial year since incorporation.

- **Original Entity:** The entity must not have been formed by splitting up or reconstructing an existing business.

- **Innovation & Scalability:** Must be working towards innovation, development, or improvement of products, processes, or services, or have a scalable business model with high potential for employment or wealth creation.

3.2. Section 80-IAC: Key Conditions for Tax Exemption

To claim the tax holiday under Section 80-IAC of the Income Tax Act:

- **Incorporation Window:** The startup must be incorporated on or after 1st April 2016 but before 1st April 2030 (subject to further extensions as per Finance Acts).

- **Entity Type:** Must be a Private Limited Company or LLP.

- **Approval Required:** Must be recognized by DPIIT and certified as eligible by the Inter-Ministerial Board (IMB).

- **Tax Benefit:** Eligible to claim 100% tax exemption on profits for any 3 consecutive years out of the first 10 years of incorporation.

- **Investment Restrictions:** Must not be substantially financed by or have invested capital from certain ineligible sources (such as foreign institutional investors or large corporates where applicable).

3.3. IMB Evaluation Approach: What They Look For

The Inter-Ministerial Board assesses applications based on qualitative parameters, including:

- **Problem-Solution Fit:** Clearly defined market problem and how the startup addresses it.

- **Innovation Quotient:** Use of new technology, novel approach, or significant process improvement.

- **Scalability:** Business model should demonstrate potential to scale nationally or globally.

- **Differentiation:** Clear USP compared to existing market solutions.

- **Impact:** Tangible potential to create employment or wealth in the Indian economy.

Rejections often stem from vague innovation claims, lack of market validation, or weak articulation of the product's impact.

3.4. Commonly Approved Industry Segments

Based on observed trends and processed applications, the following sectors often meet approval standards—provided they are backed by real innovation and impact:

- **Healthtech:** Telemedicine, AI-driven diagnostics, health analytics platforms.

- **Fintech:** Digital lending, insurtech, payment tech, credit scoring solutions.

- **Agritech:** Farm-to-consumer platforms, precision agriculture, IoT in farming.

- **Edtech:** Adaptive learning platforms, vernacular content delivery, skill-building tools.

- **Logistics & Mobility**: Last-mile optimization, EV logistics, supply chain tech.

- **SaaS & Enterprise Tech**: B2B platforms offering automation, cloud-native tools, or sector-specific solutions.

This appendix is intended to bring clarity to the regulatory landscape and highlight areas of opportunity. It reflects my practice philosophy: simplify the complex, systematize the process, and create dependable outcomes.

APPENDIX 4

SAMPLE ENGAGEMENT LETTERS AND CLIENT AGREEMENTS

These templates help professionals clearly define the scope and expectations when offering startup advisory and 80IAC services.

4.1 Sample Engagement Letter for Startup Registration

Key Clauses:

- Scope: DPIIT recognition, documentation, portal filing

- Timeline: Approx. 7–14 working days

- Fees: ₹[X] + GST, payable 50% in advance

- Client responsibilities: Timely document submission

4.2 Sample Engagement Letter for 80IAC Advisory

Key Clauses:

- Eligibility assessment

- IMB documentation preparation

- Representation in case of query or rejection

- Fees linked to phases (drafting, submission, post-submission follow-up)

4.3 Best Practices for Client Agreements

- Define non-guarantee clauses for approval outcomes

- Include confidentiality and data security terms

- Clearly mention liability caps for professional advice

Conclusion

This book has aimed to provide a practical and strategic guide for navigating the complex landscape of DPIIT recognition, 80IAC certification, and startup tax incentives. By mastering technical criteria, anticipating regulatory trends, and leveraging professional tools, both startups and their advisors can unlock significant growth and financial benefits.

Closing Note: For the CA Who Wants to Do More 

If you've read this far, you're not average.

You're looking for the next level. Whether you want to enter the startup advisory niche or partner with someone who has, I hope this book gave you clarity on what's possible.

We are standing at the edge of transformation - both in India's economy and our profession.

DPIIT, 80-IAC, and the entire Startup India ecosystem are not just schemes. They're signals of where value is being created.

"If you're a fellow CA interested in deepening your understanding or expanding into this niche, I welcome meaningful conversations. I'm always open to exchanging insights with forward-thinking peers. You can connect with me either through email (mentioned at last page) or through WhatsApp (Scan the code given at last page) for knowledge sharing.

Let's raise the bar for what Chartered Accountants can achieve in India's startup economy."

A SMALL REQUEST 

Acknowledgment of Errors: The author and publisher shall be obliged if the errors are brought to their notice to carry out corrections in future editions.

Feedback and Suggestions: For any feedback and valuable suggestions, you can mail at **ca.meghajain@outlook.com**

Connect with the Author: If you have questions or want future updates in relation to the topics covered in this book further, you can reach the Author at:

Scan QR code

WhatsApp contact